PAMELA D. SMITH

- b l a -
- c k f -
- a c e -

Personal Branding, Leadership Development, and Service Advisory Tips for Emerging Black Leaders

Randall R. Smith, Sr • Cha'Darius L. Spencer
Randall R. Smith, Jr • RaTiage J. Smith

Pamela D. Smith © 2022

All rights reserved. No part of this book may be reproduced, stored, or transmitted by any means, whether auditory, graphic, mechanical, or electronic, without written permission of both publisher and author, except in the case of brief excerpts used in articles and other noncommercial uses permitted by copyright law. Unauthorized reproduction of any part of this work is illegal and punishable by law.

ISBN-13: 978-1-7377896-4-2
ISBN E-Book: 978-1-7377896-5-9
Library of Congress Control Number: 2022906426

Visionary Author | Project Manager
Pamela D. Smith

Contributing Authors
Randall Smith, Sr. | Cha'Darius Spencer | Randall Smith, Jr. | RaTiage Smith

Book Creation & Design
DHBonner Virtual Solutions LLC
www.dhbonner.net

For bulk purchasing, email: info@pameladsmith.net

Published in the United States of America

- b l a -
- c k f -
- a c e -

Personal Branding, Leadership Development, and Service Advisory Tips for Emerging Black Leaders

tribute

To the late Samuel Modest, Jr, a great friend, a brother, and human being I called "Blackface." You demonstrated what it means to be resilient, full of life, personable, and kind.

Your black face was bold . . . and it was brave. You are forever in my heart. Continue to rest in peace.

-Randall R. Smith, Sr.

This book is for every blackface (precious, Black person) who is determined to rise above every obstacle, every setback, every hindrance, and every limitation; for those who are proud when they look in the mirror and see their black face!

You were born to lead. Serve well. Lead well.

*You are who
you believe you are!*

table of contents

INTRODUCTION	xiii
SELF SERVICE & LEADERSHIP	1
Becoming internally self-aware to lead self and build a personal brand	4
Self-Awareness Assessment	8
How do I see the fruit?	10
Intentionally Building a Personal Leadership Brand	13
Three Tips to Build your Personal Leadership Brand	15
HOME SERVICE & LEADERSHIP	21
Establish Home Values	21
Being Respectful at Home	21
Problem Solving at Home	22
A common challenge	23
COMMUNITY SERVICE & LEADERSHIP	31
Identifying gaps in Black communities	31
Being an advocate	35
CAREER/SCHOOL SERVICE & LEADERSHIP	41
Be Coachable	41
Embrace Constructive Feedback	41
Watch What You Tell Yourself	42
SOCIAL SERVICE & LEADERSHIP	47
Your Circle of Influence Matters	47
Fostering Trust Among Your Friends	47
BRAND STRATEGY FRAMEWORK	53
Personal Brand Strategy	52
Brand Analysis	55

Characteristics of your Target Audience	57
Notes	58
SAMPLE BRAND STRATEGY	61
Brand Analysis (SWOT):	61
CONCLUSION	73
RESOURCES	77
ABOUT THE AUTHORS	79
Contact	83

introduction

The world has changed... a lot... especially for African Americans. We have evolved and are making our mark in the world. We know it sounds cliché, but one month is not nearly enough time to celebrate our political, artistic, and cultural achievements. Twenty-eight days is not sufficient time to honor our triumphs as we try to move past the traumatic memories and mentions of our struggles.

This book is not meant to deny or downplay what happened to us generations ago or what we experience today. We do not debate truth. Instead, it has been written to affirm every black face's resilience, courage, confidence, and character. It explores the depth of the beauty of our color so that we can unapologetically continue to expand the legacies of those before us while building powerful and personal black brands.

Sure, there has been a stigma and a negative portrayal of African Americans. The idea of "blackface" has even

INTRODUCTION

been considered racist and offensive. "For a white person to paint his or her face black was considered a mockery of enslaved Africans. White performers in minstrel shows would paint their faces black as a form of mockery; unacceptable to say the least. Unacceptable because it invokes a racist and painful history" (Kaur, 2019).

Some of the early minstrel shows were of white performers who darkened their skin (put on a black face) to depict laziness, cowardliness, and ignorance - as Black people were seen. So, we understand the pain and gruesome agony associated with such a depiction. However, black faces come with personality, charisma, strength, perseverance, kindness, and compassion. Even the darkest shade of blackness comes with some of the brightest smiles ever seen. Smiles brighter than Behr Ultra's Pure White PR-W15 LRV94.4 paint.

Yes, we identify with the pain and offense associated with "black face," yet we also embrace the term of endearment and the strength that we see demonstrated daily on black faces.

With memories in mind and lived experiences to glean from, we want to inspire black faces, brown faces, and all faces of color who have been outcast and made to feel less than to identify with the beauty of who you are.

> Black faces are not what has been labeled.
> Black faces are not the negative pictures that have been painted.

INTRODUCTION

Black faces are fierce.

Black faces are courageous.

Black faces are unique.

Black faces are beautiful.

Black faces are royal.

Black faces are everything they were created to be.

Yes, we are all of that.

Our goal with this book is not to have you reading a bunch of fluff or even a bunch of history, but to elevate your belief in yourself and provide you with the framework to build your brand; to have you thinking better, believing bigger, and expecting more. You deserve it, and you can have it.

Although this is a short read, we want you to dedicate time to read this for your own development and empowerment. Meditate on the theme of the chapter and speak over yourself, declaring who you are. Visualize what it feels like to be experiencing a manifestation of your personal brand on a higher level (because it is possible). Embody it. Live in it on a higher level.

Removing the pain and stench associated with the mistreatment and abuse of black faces is no easy feat. Unlearning and canceling every negative thing that has been spoken over and to us is not easy, but we can do it. We can rise above it. Every thrown stone can be used to build strength, resilience, and courage, which become the foundation of a lasting brand.

INTRODUCTION

Our history has left many of us discouraged. You may even be experiencing a season of discouragement right now. Discouragement can leave you ill-equipped, disempowered, and disengaged, but we want to encourage you to get back into the fight. Let our history encourage you to go for what they said you could not have, be who they said you could not be, and do what they said you could not do.

Experiencing seasonal low points is normal. What is not normal or permissible is to stay in a low place. There is still some fight left in you; you just need to encourage yourself and remind yourself that there is a David in you that can overcome every Goliath (barrier) set up to stop you.

Will it be difficult? *Yes.*
Will it require commitment and perseverance? *Yes.*
But you are courageous.

Our definition of the word encourage is "the courage that is within." You were born courageous. You just need to go within and pull from what is already there. There is a servant leader within — one who can make an impact in an unfair, unjust world by creating an impactful personal brand.

INTRODUCTION

WE ARE BEAUTIFUL BLACK FACES!

self service & leadership

"Ninety-five percent of people think they're self-aware, but only ten to fifteen percent truly are."
-From a series of surveys by Eurich

Self-awareness helps shape your effectiveness as a Black leader.

"All them hypocrites do is lie, cheat, and steal. I cannot wait until she gets back on this line so that I can let her know that I see right through her. She belongs over yonder with the rest of the hoodlums. If I call and get another one of them on the line, I am going to take my business elsewhere."

"Awww, Linda. Give the girl a chance... she is doing better than the rest of them. At least she is trying to work to earn her living. The rest of 'em just want to take what they want."

1

I could not believe what I was hearing. I asked Mrs. Linda to hold, but I did not put her in an actual hold; I put her on mute. I only put her on mute because I was trying to be respectful and not have her listen to the sound of the keyboard as I was clicking through screens to find her information. I was trying to serve her as best as I could.

Hearing what she was saying was very disturbing. In fact, it pierced, and this piercing dropped my level of enthusiasm; I no longer had it in me to help her. I deemed it best that I transfer her call because my disappointment in what I heard her say was going to be obvious in my tone. To be honest, it was not disappointment — it was pure anger. I unmuted, and all I said was "one moment," and I did a blind transfer.

If you have ever worked in a customer service, call-center type environment, then you may have heard the term "blind transfer" being used; it is when you transfer a customer's call without making sure the person you are transferring them to will pick up. They may end up getting voicemail, and oftentimes, this angers the customer.

I know all too well because I have taken many calls when customers say, "I was talking to Agent So-and-So, and they dropped me in someone's voicemail. They could have told me they were transferring me." It is certainly not a pleasant thing to do, and it is not delivering excellent service.

I began to let out a big sigh, and before it was over, my manager was rolling his chair up to my desk.

Manager: "Do you still have Mrs. Linda on hold?"

Me: "No." (He knew I did not because he saw me sighing).

Manager: "I was doing a service observe, and you did a blind transfer. I wrote this up as a coaching opportunity. We cannot blind transfer customers like that. You were supposed to let her know that you were transferring her and give her an option to leave a voicemail or for you to come back on the line. A leader would have..."

Yada, yada, yada. He lost me at the end. When he said a leader would have, he did not say a good leader would have, an aspiring leader would have, or an emerging leader would have . . . . he just told me that I was not a leader.

Same day, different time. A team member came to my desk to share with me how a customer had yelled at her on the phone and that she had hung up on her. She proceeded to tell me that our manager was doing a service observe on her call and told her that she had done the right thing because he would have hung up on the customer also.

I desperately wanted to ask her if he told her that "a leader would have...," but I figured she probably would have told me he had said that. She would not have been so proud of her actions; instead of coming to my desk with bragging rights, she would have been coming to vent about our manager.

Wow. The black face employee did not demonstrate leadership skills because she transferred an irate customer to her representative, but the other employee demonstrated leadership skills because she hung up on a customer. And no, she never said that the manager told her that she was a leader, or a great one, or an emerging one, but he did tell her that she did the right thing. And that is what leaders do. They do the right thing.

This was the beginning of my journey into thinking that Black people, those with black faces, particularly myself as a Black woman, were not leaders. This was the beginning of my thinking that to be a leader, I would have to achieve a leadership title at a company — either someone would have to appoint me as a leader, or I would have to earn this designation. At this time, I had no idea that I was born a leader, a black face leader.

I had no self-awareness. Self-awareness is understanding what we were born to do and who we were born to be; it is a critical core value that helps a leader continue to develop. As a leader, we must constantly evolve and grow. Without doing so, we minimize the level of impact that we will have and the difference that we can make in the lives of others.

Self-awareness is more than knowing our external features or what we may or may not be physically capable of; requiring going inward and being conscious of the things we are enthusiastic about — our aspirations and values.

However, because I was not self-aware, I did not realize that I did not manage the situation as best as I could. I was not being a great servant, and that was my weakness. Still, my strength was that I was not any of the stereotypes or labels Mrs. Linda had given me. I was not a liar. I had not even given her any information about her account for her to think I had not told her the truth. Cheating and stealing?

Okay, Mrs. Linda. You took my power that day, but no one ever can in that way again.

I realized my potential after I let out "the sigh." I was exhaling what she said and not allowing it to stick. Then, to add insult to injury, my manager *attempted* to affirm what the customer had said without saying it; at least, that is how I perceived it, and perception is everything.

Now, self-awareness is two-fold, so it is possible to be externally self-aware without being internally self-aware.

becoming internally self-aware to lead self and build a personal brand

To become internally self-aware, we must be open-minded. Servant leaders are not closed-minded; we are mindful of our strengths and weaknesses, we are disciplined, and we set boundaries.

Why are things like understanding our strengths and weaknesses, being disciplined, and having boundaries so prime? Because before we can serve with excellence and lead effectively, we must start with self. Self? Yes, with self.

Black faces (Black people) do not always make self-care a priority. We are good with self-maintenance, which is what so many confuse with self-care. I did for years. As a black-faced female leader, I considered things like getting my hair and nails done, the monthly massages that I still get, and eating at expensive restaurants were deemed self-care. I was doing all of these things, yet for so many years, I was still extremely overwhelmed, gaining a lot of weight, and lacking clarity in my purpose. What a relief it was when I understood self-care and how being self-aware helped me to take better care of me.

To serve with excellence and be an effective Black leader, I had to start setting boundaries. You must do the same. Those boundaries begin with self. We must stop breaking the promises we make to self. We must stop being silent when it is time to speak and stop speaking when it is time to be silent. We must learn to be bold in our beliefs while still being respectful in our communication.

- Internal self-awareness is understanding that for every promise we break to ourselves, we lower our standards and begin to accept things that are not in alignment with what we really want.

- Internal self-awareness is understanding that when we are silent when we should be speaking, we are not expressing ourselves; this gives others the permission to be disrespectful in their communication with us, and we nonverbally communicate that we are in agreement with what they are saying. When we speak when we should be silent, we are not preserving our energy and effectively using our communication skills.

- Internal self-awareness is understanding that being bold in our beliefs while still being respectful in our communication means it is okay to stand firm on what we believe, even if we are standing alone. And it is okay to communicate our beliefs with the understanding that others have a right to believe differently. That communication should always be seasoned with love, respect, and grace.

All servant leaders are self-aware. All black-faced servant leaders are self-aware. We serve and lead, and we do it just as well or effectively as anyone else. Sure, I was supposed to let Mrs. Linda know that I was transferring her call. Some may feel as if I was supposed to continue servicing her, but I beg to differ. No school, no job, and no organization should expect you to lay dormant in the face of verbal abuse, racial slurs, and discrimination. If you are being asked to proceed in a comparable situation, then you need to take this up the chain.

Being self-aware does not mean you allow everything.

It means you know what your weakness is; mine, in this scenario, was my failure to conduct excellence in service (by telling her that she was being transferred and if she received voicemail, she could leave a message or press zero to speak to a different representative). Although I was not going to go any further than that with Mrs. Linda, ending it that way would have been equally professional and powerful. By the way I terminated it, she knew she got under my skin; my black skin. If only she could have seen the expression on my black face!

My other weakness was not expressing to my manager how he made me feel and how I felt as if he was not advocating for me. If he heard my response, surely he heard the things she was saying about me.

Some may say, "She did not mean for you to hear that. She thought you had her on hold." It was just a moment of truth and expression that was revealed. She could not hold her private thoughts, and if she really had no intentions of me knowing her private thoughts, she would have waited until she hung up with me to express herself in the privacy of her home. In most service environments, where there is voice-to-voice customer interaction, customers are warned that calls may be monitored or recorded for quality assurance and training purposes; it was no different in this environment. As a result, I was trained. I was coached. And I became more self-aware than ever.

Let us see how self-aware you are.

self-awareness assessment

- How would you have handled the situation? Would you have a) ignored what Mrs. Linda said, b) let her know that you were transferring her call and provided her with options once transferred, or c) confronted the customer?

Answer:

- How would you have handled your manager? a) kept silent, b) told him how he made you feel, c) went to his manager about it?

Answer:

- How would you have responded to your team member? a) told her that she was wrong? b) lending your support by listening and keeping silent? c) b) told her about your experience?

Answer:

SELF-AWARENESS SCORE:

If you answered all A's:

You need to be more internally self-aware. You do not have boundaries in place, and this will only lead to frustration for you. Once frustrated, you will start to resent the people you did not set boundaries with.

If you answered all B's:

You are self-aware. Fantastic job! Keep in mind that self-awareness is a core value and a part of personal development, which is a lifelong, rewarding journey. You, the school you attend, your peers, your community, and anyone who encounters you will benefit greatly from your personal development.

If you answered all C's:

You may be self-aware, but you need to establish some restraints and protocol... and remain professional. These actions may not necessarily be wrong; however, they may not be the best choice either. Frequently in a school or work environment, there is a chain of command, and it must be followed.

Leading your own life means setting standards and embracing core values that you follow. You are constantly self-correcting as you go.

How you lead yourself and serve yourself is essential, as it sets the tone for how you will serve and lead others. This means being intentional about learning, applying knowledge, goal setting, and executing your goals. The habits you have in your life will show up in your academic studies, career habits, and business; there is no separation — meaning that you can not lead a lousy life and think you will be a great student, a great professional, a great entrepreneur, a great ministry, or great community leader.

You will only be able to navigate poor habits temporarily; eventually, those habits will stand loud and bold and sabotage the very things you are working so diligently towards. Therefore, leading starts with self. I hope I have already convinced you that you were born to lead. You just must cultivate, expand, and nourish those inner leadership characteristics so that you can see the fruit.

how do i see the fruit?

The fruit is ripened, where self-leadership is concerned, by:

1. Removing our own personal biases toward self
2. Being forgiving towards self and society
3. Maximizing your strengths and improving your weaknesses

Young, Black music artists and producers are judged harshly. Many are not looked upon as leaders but perceived as foolish. Unfair, to say the least. The music is often a coping mechanism, a cover of pain. The music becomes therapy because many were raised that "men don't cry," and therapy is "telling all of your business to a stranger." So, writing, singing, and rapping lyrics are symbolic of the tears they would have shed or how they would have expressed themselves in a therapy session.

This is not to say that young, black face music artists are the only ones who have faced trauma or the only ones who have been judged harshly or unfairly, but the outcasting makes it a double whammy. They are leaders indeed. They are self-leaders with enormous potential who often use music as a pathway to lead them into their greater purpose. To be a music artist, you must be a self-starter, motivated, artistic, and creative. All of these are characteristics of a leader; a great, innovative leader.

Randall R. Smith, Jr. is no stranger to judgment, criticism, lies, and trauma. He is also no stranger to injustice and police profiling. His courageous spirit and unashamed misfortunes make him an ideal leader for himself and his peers. He believes that there is power in sharing your story, and one should do so without fear of judgment, criticism, or shame. "Your mistakes and misfortunes become someone else's wisdom and life lessons. In sharing your story, you are using your voice to mentor others," he shares.

Leaders share their stories and allow others to learn

from the things they have gone through — whether self-inflicted or through no fault of their own. Your story becomes a part of your personal brand, and it is what connects you with others who share a similar experience.

* * *

Randall R. Smith, Jr.

As a leader, it is prime to start with leading self. When we start with leading self, it is easier to lead others. You are leading from experience when you start with self. You are not doing something that you have just learned from a book, but you are doing something that you were an active participant in. Teaching from self-experience is easier than reading or watching something and teaching it.

When I look at a person's life, there are things that I notice about them that tell me if they are leading self well. When I see self-respect and respect for others, I see a self-leader. I know that if a person does not respect themselves, then there will be minimal to no respect for others. I also listen to the self-talk. Leaders encourage themselves. If I hear a person putting themselves down, then I know that their conversation with others may not be as encouraging and uplifting as it should as a leader. How you carry yourself in one way is how you carry yourself in any way.

intentionally building a personal leadership brand

Randall Jr's life is one reason that, as a leader, building a personal brand is salient. Well, let me say that being *intentional* about building a personal brand is salient. We are all building personal brands, whether we are intentional about it or not.

For example, a single mother probably is not aware she is building a personal brand. She probably thinks that there is not much to her life other than raising her children (which, by the way, a brand as a mother is a hell of a brand to build). She probably thinks that there is nothing special about what she is doing because she is not bringing any money into her home. She is wrong.

Her personal brand as a single mother is being built. There are people who know that she is a single mother. There are people who watch how she parents her children. There are people who see things like the meals that she prepares, the discipline she is instilling in her children, and the structure she has built within her home. When those who know her and about all the moving parts that it takes to be a mother and how she does it with ease and grace — hear the term single mother — she likely comes to mind.

Why does she come to mind? Because she is building a personal brand as a single mother, she is an example to other single mothers. She is a leader. She is not intentional about it; she is just doing what she does, creating a positive image in the mind of others of how being a single mother is not the end of the world. She has created a positive impression that a single mother can be successful, even if that success is in none other than how well she parents her children.

Let us consider a young college student who does not think they are building a personal brand. Throughout their early education years, they were always late turning in homework, they would study the day prior to a test, not take good notes in class, and their grades suffered. They enrolled in college because they heard that college was easier than high school and had less oversight. In their minds, college would be a breeze because less oversight meant that they would not have an instructor standing over their back, asking them about homework all the time.

To their surprise, their grades start to suffer in college too. They are unaware that this academic record is a part of their personal brand. When their name is mentioned in their academic department, they may be known as the student who is not diligent in their studies, the one who is not applying themselves, or the one who is barely getting by. This is a personal brand. One that they, themselves, are building.

Of course, it can be self-corrected by changing their mindset, habits, and work ethics, but this demonstrates how we are building a personal brand, whether we are doing so intentionally or unintentionally.

Pamela D. Smith

three tips to build your personal leadership brand

- **Intentionally Build:** You are building a personal brand anyway, so it is to your advantage to do so intentionally. Be concerned with how others see you, what they think about you, and what they say when you are not in the room. By building intentionally, you are setting yourself up for better opportunities, positioning yourself as the leader you are, and becoming an influencer among your peers.

- **Take Inventory:** Consider the things you are passionate about and become an advocate for them. Each of us has something that we are passionate about, something we want to see changed, better, or eliminated. As a personal brand, you have a powerful voice. Use it to serve and make others better.

- **Teach Others:** Share what you know. Stop thinking you do not know enough. You know enough to help someone else. If someone is struggling in a class or an area of life that you are excelling in, offer to tutor, mentor, or give them tips and hold them accountable for implementing the strategies provided.

* * *

Randall R. Smith, Jr.

Personal branding is a reflection of your personal purpose and personal ideas and values. It is the image that you have built of yourself. I am in the 21-25 age group; most of my peers are not intentionally building a personal brand, but I do believe that they are becoming more aware of how they want to be seen amongst their peers. The age when leaders are becoming aware that building a personal brand is esteemed is younger.

As young black face men, we are judged, stereotyped, and profiled. This makes it even more critical to build a positive personal brand. You want to make those assumptions and judgments not true. Yes, we are all human, so there is a capacity for error in each of us, but the overall image you want to intentionally build will triumph over any mistakes or mishaps.

We also face barriers, but that is why we must tap into the leader within and stand in our power and greatness. Being intentional about building a personal brand helps us stand in that power and greatness. What we do will outlast what we say we can do.

It starts with forgiving those who have wronged or misjudged us. If we are walking around with grudges, we are taking away from our own creativity. That energy is not being best used. A grudge is too heavy, and carrying one means you are unintentionally building a brand of unforgiveness. Holding on takes away the power and greatness we were born with as black face leaders. Yes, be aware of who is trying to limit us and who is trying to hold us back, but that should not stop us from creating and dominating in our lane.

When we are self-aware, we know when we have slacked. We know when we are not doing our best. Be aware, and do not make the limitations an idol. Build on your strengths. Improve on your weakness.

Black face, to me, means a Black person who is a leader; a strong, Black, industrious individual. One who may have had many barriers stacked against them but still push forward to achieve their goals; one who gets up every day to achieve their goals, although they may have to work harder than those without black faces; one who keeps going despite challenges.

BLACK FACE QUOTES

"Black face, never let judgment disrupt your journey."

"Stay positive with your time."

"Work hard and stay strong."

"Always move with love and respect."

"*I am Randall R. Smith, Jr.*, and my Black Face is ambitious and respectful."

home service & leadership

*"Belief in oneself and knowing who you are,
I mean, that's the foundation for everything great."*
-Jay Z

There tends to be a myth surrounding African American men, suggesting that they are less involved in their family lives. But this stereotype has been repeatedly proven to be untrue. Although many Black women are not married when they get pregnant, most Black men engage in raising their children.

As fathers raise their children, it is imperative that they teach their children how to lead within the home. The growth and development of young Black men and girls in the home are integral to becoming leaders in life because valuable morals, qualities, and characteristics can be developed to help establish one's personal brand as an emerging Black leader. Here are some ways being a leader at home can help you become the strong Black leader you want to be.

establish home values

Without values, it is difficult to be an efficient leader since your personal brand will not have direction or purpose. Establishing your personal values is an essential part of becoming a leader, and you can instill these values early on within a family setting. For example, you may decide that loyalty is crucial to you since you were loyal to your siblings growing up.

As young Black faces in high school, college, or even entry-level positions, you will encounter situations where you will start to establish what is essential to you. You may want to adopt core values that include loyalty, honesty, responsibility, and fairness.

being respectful at home

A great quality for any leader is always to be respectful. You can practice this as a leader in your home by having self-respect and treating others within your family with respect. A home setting is a perfect place to practice being respectful since it is likely that you will disagree with your family members and with some of the home rules at times. However, even though you disagree, you will still need to treat the people in your home and the rules of the house with respect.

It is highly valuable to learn to treat — even those you disagree with — respectfully because you will face plenty of conflict outside of the home. You will still need to treat your other team members, school peers, or employees with respect in these situations.

problem solving at home

As an emerging Black leader, it is crucial to be able to problem-solve; you will probably come across demanding situations. You will need to be a strong leader that can create solutions that benefit all parties.

Problem-solving is an essential skill that also includes suggesting peaceful resolutions. If you are still in that type of home, you can practice problem-solving by helping your siblings or parents. If you are in your own home, you know that the burden of problem-solving rests upon your shoulder, so you will need to know how to resolve conflict or be innovative when problems arise.

Randall R. Smith, Sr.

As a Black face leader in my home, there are challenges that are faced. These challenges cause one to look within and often require men to build up their confidence, lifestyle changes, and managerial skills.

Pamela D. Smith

a common challenge

Black face men may encounter the challenge of having a Black spouse who is independent. It can be challenging to get your spouse to let her guard down and allow you to lead. One of the most effective ways to do this is by demonstrating the ability to lead by being accountable and following through on what you say you will do. This applies if you are not yet married and living on your own.

If you are in school and living with your parents, you will still need to be accountable and follow through on what you say you are going to do. If you cannot do this at home, you will find it challenging to be able to do it in the marketplace.

It is depressing to work hard on a job while being passed over for promotions; promotions you know you deserve are given to white counterparts who have not worked as hard as you have, and the production speaks to that. Developing tough skin should start at home to be equipped for things like this on the job or at school because it does happen.

Societal challenges can make it difficult for life at home. When you go out into the world every day and are treated differently because you know what you know, you are viewed as being strong — not just physically, but in character and knowledge. The stereotype of Black men being lazy stems from the fact that some Black men have given up on the workforce.

This does not mean that Black men are not working; it

just means that some are not giving it their all on a job, in their career, or in school because they have experienced giving it their all, and it was not deemed good enough. Being overlooked for promotions that you know you qualify for; being excluded from greater opportunities; not receiving equal pay . . . all of this creates inner struggle and has the potential to be carried over into the home life. However, leading at home means that the joy and peace of your family take priority over what has happened to you in the world, in the workforce, or at school.

Once you are at home, you must remember that you are amongst people who love, appreciate, celebrate, and honor you. They do not deserve to have the frustration that outside has caused you to be brought inside. No one will look at you as a leader if you are always angry, not a joy to be around, and leading from a hostile place; you will not be looked at as a leader in your home if this is how you are.

This also applies to single mothers. If you are the leader in your home, then your children do not deserve for you to allow your job to frustrate you, and that frustration is brought home. You are sowing discord within your home, teaching them to allow outside influences to disturb their inner peace.

It took me a while to get over being fired from a job I was giving my all to. I was a diligent worker, receiving lots of positive feedback, training new temporary employees, and putting in extra hours. One day, I was approached by a senior leader who advised that he had been watching me all day and felt that I should have completed more than what I had. I respectfully replied, "If you have been watching me all day, then you know the chain keeps breaking. I am not behind on production; I just have not completed what I normally would have." I could tell that he did not like my reply. I was polite in my tone but was told by my immediate manager (who was also white) that the senior manager did not like that I just did not say, "Okay, I'll speed up," so he labeled me as confrontational.

One month later, I was terminated. My immediate manager was shocked and disappointed. He stated that I was the best on his team, and he was honest enough to say that the senior manager had not appreciated my reply.

It is devastating that black faces are expected to be so submissive that their voices cannot be heard. I was only explaining to the senior manager why I was not exceeding in my production on that day, and he did not like something about that, so it cost me my job, which can cause a lot of stress in the home. Being fired can be mentally heavy. Imagine if I did not have a wife who was also a leader and supportive. When I say leader, I am not talking about a management position, but about a person's character and how they move past opposition and stand strong in their home and other areas.

Knowing how to lead well in your home, deal with adversity, and persevere helps you do the same in society. This will help you build a brand that is not solely financially dependent on someone else — a brand where your financial future is not controlled by someone else.

Does this mean that you should not work for anyone else? Absolutely not! It means that no one else should have the power over your finances. It means you build a personal and professional brand that will have others advocating for you, and your brand will help open doors for you.

Leading in the home means leading by example. As a parent, I have conversations with my children. If you are a parent, you should be having conversations with your children. Conversations with your children should be about sharing lessons. If you are not a parent, then discussions with your parents should include receiving wisdom from the lessons they have learned. I always share with my children that when they see an opportunity to do better . . . take it. Always try to "sow" what you want to reap, and I do not just mean financially.

Black families have it harder than others, simply due to the color of our skin. Black fathers must deal with things that non-Black fathers do not. Black children must deal with things other children do not. This makes home life hard for black faces. As a leader in my home, I try not to be too hard on my children, as I understand what they must deal with in society. When they make a mistake, I do not make them feel bad about the error. Yes, I want them to learn the lesson, but I do not guilt-trip them.

It is vital for me — and should be for you — to be looked upon as a leader in your home before being concerned with being looked upon as a leader anywhere else. Being a home leader means providing for the family members, telling others within the household what is right and wrong, showing my children how to prosper, and teaching them how to be kind and helpful to others.

Being a leader in the home is imperative because black faces need to have someone to look up to. It is also important to be a leader in breaking generational patterns. Some things have been passed down to black faces that make it hard for us to live like others, a mindset that needs to be challenged, uprooted, and changed.

I must be a leader in my home so that my spouse has someone dependable that she and my children can rely on. As she is a valuable Black woman, I want to make sure that I am shouldering responsibilities and not giving her more things to worry about. I want to make sure that I support her in fulfilling her goals and dreams.

However, maybe you are not married. Perhaps you are still in school or just beginning your career. It is just as vital for you to be a leader in your home to give your parents less to worry about. Your parents should be able to trust that when they send you off to school, you will be responsible and not waste their money. They should be able to trust that you are not going to get sidetracked by the things that will be offered to you that may take your focus.

A leader is trustworthy. It does not matter your age or what home life is like for you; you are a leader, and building a positive personal brand means being trustworthy.

BLACK FACE QUOTES

"Live and Let Live."

"Where one won't, one will."
(Do not let anyone hinder your progress.)

"Stay down (solid) until you come up."

"Seems like something."
(Things are getting better.)

"I am *Randall R. Smith, Sr.*,
and my Black face is loyalty and strength."

community service & leadership

> *"The only way you can really see change is by helping create it."*
> -Lena Waithe

We, the people, acknowledge that we have come a long way, yet still have a long way to go. Thus, it is critical that we come together as a community and show support to each other. Doing it occasionally is not nearly enough to move the needle forward.

When we say "come together as a community of Black faces," this does not mean we oppose or come against any other racial group. It simply means we realize the need for diversity to be embraced, recognize the need for unity amongst our community, and understand that there are gaps that lock us out of opportunities, representation, and advancement. Community service and leadership serve the purpose of collaborating with community members to facilitate problem-solving and create innovation that will benefit the black faces. As an emerging leader, part of building your personal brand is community involvement. It does not matter what your role in society is; you can contribute to your community in several ways:

- Find out the concerns of your community.
- Find out what changes the community members would like to see.
- Find out how you can contribute to change.

Understand that community does not only mean the neighborhood that you live in. It is great to be involved in that as well; however, it is imperative to find different Black communities that you can add value to for the advancement of black faces — as well as build your personal brand, develop as a leader, and provide service to Black people.

identifying gaps in black communities

There are educational communities.
There are financial communities.
There are leadership opportunity communities.
There are equal justice communities.
There are youth communities.
There are equal employment communities.
There are equal housing communities.

There is a substantial gap in educational achievement for Black faces. Some may argue that the gap is due to a lack of will and effort; however, research shows that the gap is primarily due to unequal access to educational resources. "In fact, the U.S. educational system is one of the most unequal in the industrialized world, and students routinely receive dramatically different learning opportunities based on their social status" (Darling-Hammond, 1998).

A way to serve your community and lead them to change is by becoming a tutor in urban areas. Another way is to teach the importance of education, narrow the gap, or start a school drop-out prevention program.

Cha'Darius was an A and B student who consistently won awards for his academic achievement. One year, he collected seven awards during his school's end-of-the-year program. He was awarded in every category that an award was given. He continued to excel at this level until high school. This was when the family relocated to Houston, Texas. His rebellion against the move mentally caused him to check out of his academics, as coping with the move was extremely hard for him — he had developed friendships back in his hometown, and moving was not a part of his plan. The move was a culture shock.

Coming from a small city where everything is structured, his parents worked only five minutes away from home, and he had his grandmother, aunt, and uncles less than a mile away. The city life was different, and the schools certainly were. They were overcrowded, and it seemed as if the kids were left alone to tend to themselves after school, leaving opportunities to become involved in the wrong things.

To avoid it all, he started skipping school; however, unbeknownst to his parents, he would leave for the bus station, and once they were gone to work, he would go back home. His parents never found out until a neighbor informed them. The neighbor came home early from work one day and discovered that his child, along with a few other children (Cha'Darius included) in the neighborhood, was skipping. Suddenly, the truancy letters started coming in, and the fines piled up. Going from being an honor roll student to a truant one was a multi-layered problem:

- Working parents — with mom having a long commute to and from work
- A lack of Black teachers in the educational system who understood and cared (or caring teachers overall)
- Rebellion against the move
- Having a challenging time adjusting to new people
- and his own decision to start skipping school

The above concerns led to his relocating to Louisiana with his grandmother and enrolling in a GED program, which he completed in less than a month, although the program was four months. Based on this, it can be said that education is essential to him, but he did not adjust well to the move, so he decided not to become a part of the city culture and did something different. He is to be commended for deciding that education was significant enough for him to enroll in a GED program, complete the program, and later enroll in college.

Oftentimes, we look at the ones who followed the perfect societal path as leaders, but we should also consider those who veered off but thought it critical enough to create their own path and still end up at the same destination. Cha'Darius believes that community service and leadership are vital in helping to shape the younger members of communities.

* * *

Cha'Darius L. Spencer

It is essential to have a positive community image if you want others to follow you. Community leaders discourage community members from following negativity.

When I look for examples of someone who is a community leader, I see intelligence; I see someone giving back to their community, whether financially or in the form of education. I also see a community leader as one who is not taking from their community but giving back in different ways. People are also looked upon as community leaders if they are family-oriented. Those who deem their own families as meaningful understand that serving their community helps strengthen other families.

Being an influencer in your community means that you need to develop a strong, personal brand. When your brand is built, you can influence more people. You can build your brand through community leadership by being aware of what is affecting your community, speaking on relatable topics regarding your community, and providing your expertise and solutions to those issues.

being an advocate

An advocate is someone who supports a cause. We need more Black-faced advocates in our communities, especially our financial community. "Even before the Covid-19 pandemic, the 2019 national Black poverty rate was more than double the white poverty rate in the U.S. (roughly 22% compared to 9%, respectively), as reported by the Kaiser Family Foundation (KFF)." (Opara, 2022)

Black faces have higher student loan debt. Black faces make far less than their white counterparts, and Black women even less. These, among other factors, have led to the racial wealth gap. Therefore, community leaders are needed. Therefore, financial service by way of financial literacy is paramount. Advocating. Empowering. Educating.

* * *

Cha'Darius L. Spencer

I am seeing a lot more personal brand building in the Black community within my age group of 26-30. I attribute this to the rise of entrepreneurship and the advancement in technology.

We do not see it at the rate that we would like to because we often do not witness enough examples of someone who is financially stable and serving their community. This leaves many to believe that it cannot be done. We need more real-life examples. We need more education about branding and leadership.

There is a lack of mentors. We do not have enough community leaders teaching how it should be done, and sometimes, when you find those two or three people, their price is so high it turns you off from wanting to be educated and mentored by them. I am not suggesting that community leaders should do everything for free. That is not realistic. I am not even saying that the responsibility should rest on the shoulders of a few. It should be a joint effort. However, with whatever community you are serving, part of your brand strategy should be pricing that reflects the ability of that segment of people to be able to afford the service.

I am striving to be a beacon of light in my community. For those who want to follow that lead, we must be intentional about creating a positive image, being realistic with our community, and educating ourselves so that we can impart knowledge to others. We need to know what is happening around us and how everyone is affected. We need to support the efforts of those in our communities who are also leading and trying to have influence. We also must remove all judgment. It is not good to not be doing anything yourself, yet criticizing someone who is trying.

I am honored to be Black. When I think of the word 'black face,' or even when I see a black face, I see someone living their truth.

I am a music artist, and with that comes a lot of judgment and stereotyping. I would contribute this to other races not having a proper understanding of what we have been through and understanding that music is an expression; it is an art. I am proud that, for the most part, the Black community supports music artists. They acknowledge the gift as they would any other gift. They do not judge the fact that the expression may not always be as clean as one would like it to be because they understand that the pain that many black faces have endured has not always been clean. We must frequently keep it real and poetically express it exactly the way it feels.

* * *

Black Face Quotes

"Black faces are resilient.
We make the impossible possible."

"High work ethics equal success."

"Stay positive, even through negative situations."

"Move with respect and knowledge."

"I am *Cha'Darius L. Spencer,*
and my Black face is diligent and creative."

career/school service & leadership

"Leadership is not a position or a title; it is an action and example."

-unknown

Branding is one of the best ways for employees and students to make a name for themselves. Just think of iconic slogans, such as Subway's "Eat Fresh" or Nike's "Just do it." However, branding is not just for large companies. It is also incredibly considerable for individuals to establish a personal brand.

Building your personal brand is vital to how other professionals see you in the business world. A personal brand shows precisely what qualities make you unique and why clients and other working professionals should work with you. You can demonstrate your skills, strengths, and passions in your personal brand. This will help set you apart as an authority figure, which is important as an emerging Black leader.

When creating a personal brand through career leadership, it is necessary to focus on a core value. Pick a characteristic or trait that you want to emphasize about yourself; be consistent with your words and actions. For example, if you're going to be seen as reliable, you should be willing to put in the effort to help others when they could use extra support. After consistently showing your skill or worth, people will begin to view you as a reliable colleague, willing to help in times of need.

be coachable

When you first start climbing up the corporate ranks, it is critical to be coachable. Take all the advice you can get about the corporate sphere and apply it to how you build your personal brand. Being coachable is a skill that can help you quickly improve. To get the most out of your professional experiences, ask lots of questions, put in the work, and be willing to learn. You should also take inspiration from other leaders and professionals who have more experience.

embrace constructive feedback

As Black leaders in corporate America, it is grave to stand our ground and maintain our decisions as a leader, but it is also essential to embrace constructive feedback. Constructive feedback can make you a better leader and help you improve and adapt your leadership style. When you get advice on what you can do better, genuinely think about the suggestions and see if you can incorporate them into your professional career.

Embracing constructive feedback is good for your professional growth, which also helps your personal brand. Other professionals in the industry will recognize you as a professional and that you are receptive to feedback. After all, it is hard to grow when you are not.

watch what you tell yourself

It can sometimes be difficult for Black leaders in corporate settings to feel secure, but you can encourage yourself through your inner dialogue. Your internal dialogue is what you tell yourself throughout the day. Be positive when thinking about your career and know that no matter how black faces have been stereotyped, there is greatness in you. Speak it to yourself and over yourself. Believe that you are a problem solver. Believe in your ability. Be confident in your worth. Once you believe in yourself, others will feel your confidence and believe in you as well.

It took me years to realize that coaching is a gift. Early in my career, I perceived feedback and coaching as a personal attack; I interpreted these as a measurement of my ability. It took the guidance of a career mentor to tell me to pay attention to the feedback and make the necessary adjustments if I wanted to advance.

For one, when feedback is not embraced, and leaders see no growth, it becomes a part of my personal brand. I did not want to be known as a disgruntled employee who was only collecting a paycheck and had little to no interest in growing personally or professionally. My mentor shared that she could only get as far as she had in her career because she embraced the feedback.

Coaching will not always feel good, and at times, may be a hard pill to swallow, but it is designed to help you understand where you are, your strengths, and in what areas you need to grow.

BLACK FACE QUOTES

"Black faces make valuable use of
the information and resources that are available to you.
That is how you keep elevating."

"The quality of your life reflects
the choices that you make."

"Empowerment is you no longer
being enslaved to your past."

"Stand in your truth, even if it's not
what others want for you."

I am *Pamela D. Smith,*
and my Black face is resilient and endearing.

social service & leadership

*"Do not follow the crowd.
Let the crowd follow you."*
-Margaret Thatcher

Social leadership is essential to developing your persona when building a personal brand. It helps to define who you are within a social setting. As society becomes more empathetic, social leadership skills become necessary to effectively lead others so as not to follow a crowd that is leading you nowhere.

Social leadership is when you establish authority amongst your peers/friends/social circle through your personal brand and reputation. The authority you develop among social groups can benefit your personal brand since it will help you be recognized for your strong social skills. You can achieve social leadership through practicing humility, kindness, and treating others with respect.

It is crucial to have social leadership skills that can help you resolve solutions and make decisions in complex environments. Social leadership is even more important in this new age of technology. There are now new ways to gain social influence, such as utilizing social media and becoming a social influencer.

your circle of influence matters

Your circle of influence is the people you surround yourself with and interact with regularly. This can include your children, relatives, friends, classmates, and coworkers. Your circle of influence is vital in creating your personal brand since they influence your values and views in life. Habits and environment are two main factors determining who you become; therefore, surrounding yourself with successful, confident people can subconsciously shape your personality.

The people around you play a huge role in your motivations and behavior since you spend the most time with them. Within your circle of influence, you should also try to improve your social skills and learn to lead within a social setting. This is where you will practice most of the leadership skills that will be beneficial in all aspects of your life, including business.

fostering trust among your friends

In any relationship, whether with friends, family, or coworkers, you should always create a sense of trust. Trust is a crucial part of relationships since it allows each person to feel like they can rely on one another.

When it comes to Black leadership in a social group, you need to trust your peers while they trust you so that you can be an effective leader. To foster trust, you should work on being more vulnerable and showing that you can allow the other person to take responsibility. Over time, you can ask them to do more tasks, showing that you know that the person is dependable and trustworthy.

They always say that "trust is a two-way street," and it is entirely true! So, by fostering trust by staying true to your word and showing your friends that you will be there for them when they need you, they will remain true to their word and demonstrate trust to you as well. Building trust is an integral part of social leadership since your friends will trust you to make the right decisions for them; they will see you taking a leadership role and advising them, which will inspire them to do the right thing.

RaTiage has experienced the adverse effects of being in the wrong crowd. The "follow the leader" mentality proved not to be wise. He quickly had to adjust his mindset to realize that there was a leader within himself; he needed to activate it by being the positive influencer in his social circle and standing up for what was right, even if he had to stand alone.

Pamela D. Smith

* * *

RaTiage J. Smith

I have played "follow the leader" and been led down paths that were not good for me or those who meant something to me, which was costly and time-consuming. I had to learn the hard way that followers do not know where they are going. They do not have clear direction or insight because they are being led by someone else — often by someone who does not even know where they are going.

Now, I am at a stage in my life when my circle of influence matters greatly. I must ask myself, "How are these people contributing to what I am trying to build as an artist and a digital music promoter?" When I say contribute, it does not mean financially; it means having people around who will enhance the mission to lead and love — people who support what I am doing and the direction I am trying to go in.

Being a leader in your social circle requires you to stand up for what is right, maintain a balance in your professional and personal life, be brave with standing firm on your decisions when you know they are the right thing to do, and be considerate of others. Especially since your environment can play a part in how influential you are.

And, although you will not always be able to change your environment, it is good to remember that with a transformative growth mindset, you can persevere and position yourself as a leader in *any* environment. Thus, it will come down to your individual mindset and choices.

* * *

BLACK FACE QUOTES

"Black faces have infinite ability."

"Life is a combination of simple and complex, but being agile is the key to persevering."

"There's always much more to what meets the eye."

"In spite of adversity, never give up. Believe for better."

I am *RaTiage J. Smith*,
and my Black face is spontaneous and innovative.

brand strategy framework

Now that you have some tips on how to lead and service "self" in your home, community, career or educational setting, and social circle, it is time to build out your brand strategy. This is the blueprint by which you start or expand your brand. It is particularly influential to do so as a Black student, career professional, entrepreneur, ministry personnel, or community leader. It is even necessary if you have decided that you will be a stay-at-home mom or dad. Your personal brand is significant.

This framework is not all-inclusive; therefore, feel free to make adjustments based on your goals and the direction you want to take your personal brand.

personal brand strategy

Defining your target audience/readers/customers should be done by identifying the average age, gender, and even race that you are targeting. You will also need to know what your target requires.

For example, if you are a student and are building your personal brand in an educational setting, you will need to understand what the academic institution requires. Once you are clear on that, you can establish your core values around those requirements. Suppose the institution requires grades of C and above, academic honesty, and being a leader amongst your peers. In that case, you need to demonstrate that you study and are concerned about your grades, you do not cheat on tests nor allow others to complete assignments for you, and you act in a way where other students consider you a positive example.

If you are a corporate professional, you should know your company's core values and align yours with the corporation's. If one of the core values of the company is customer excellence and retention, then you should make sure that each time you service a customer, you are being polite, professional, and even initiative-taking.

I am an author, my husband is a t-shirt designer, and my sons are music artists and talent developers. All of these are personal brands. My core values for my personal brand are high quality, educational, and inspirational. So, to live my core values, every book that I write or every service that I provide should be of high quality, inspirational, and educational. When you read one of my books, book me to speak, or request one of my services, you should have an experience when you learn something and are inspired. You should also receive high quality. You should not expect to book me to speak, and I show up late, I am not engaged while I am front and center speaking, and the information I share is not of value; to do this would not be to deliver on my brand values.

Brand values are how you connect with your target audience. You and your audience will share the same values, which is how you connect and become relatable. I have met a lot of Black professionals who did not understand how fundamental building a personal brand is — largely because, as Black Faces, we do not have the information and resources available to us as others may have. We also lack mentors who we can identify within the corporate, entrepreneurial, and community space.

As you are identifying your target audience, you should study your competition. Study to learn, not imitate, or make yourself feel less than. If someone is doing the same thing you are doing, you should study what they are doing, how they are doing it, and what is missing from their brand. You will make yourself stand out if there is a need in the market and your competing brands are not filling that need. You can fill the gap and have a competitive advantage in the marketplace.

This applies to an educational setting as well. What are other students not doing that is needed at the institution? You can start doing that very thing and instantly set yourself apart — becoming the influencer, the authority, the expert… the ONE!

brand analysis

A "Brand Analysis" is when you look at the brand that you have built, or the one you want to build, and ask yourself:

- What are my strengths?
- What are my weaknesses?
- What are my opportunities?
- What are my threats?

My personal brand is faith-based, so I analyze it a little differently. I ask myself:

- What has God told me to do?
- For whom has He called to tell me to do this?
- What do I have at my disposal that I can get started on and trust God along the way with what I do not have?
- What roadblocks do I foresee that I need to pray against so that I can move forward?

Yes, building a personal brand requires thought and research. There has been a rise in entrepreneurship, and it will continue to increase. Many want promotions in their jobs or to be influential in their community. We are hoping that you desire one of these. Yet, most do not take the time to build on a solid foundation — which is starting a personal brand. Yes, it is work. Yes, it requires intentionality. But it is so worth it.

I have served as a self-publishing consultant, and the one thing that vexes me is the number of authors I have worked with who are so excited about publishing their book, who spend time and money to have it done, and once their family and friends stop buying, they stop marketing their books. They spend no time prior to the release of the book to build a personal brand. Therefore, after only a few weeks of book sales, they give up because, somewhere, we have been led to believe that others will buy it just because we post that we have something for sale — not realizing that a lot of people will not even see our promotions, and those who do, do not have a connection with the brand.

So, they are not going to buy it.

If I could only tell you one thing about building a personal brand, especially one thing where a Black person is the face of the brand, it would be not to rush it. Authors, music artists, t-shirt salespersons, and many brands feel that they must buy into the trending social media timelines and build it fast. Truthfully, if you put in the necessary work and research, it will not be built fast. In fact, a personal brand is not something where there is a timeframe because it is constantly evolving.

Therefore, if we are on earth, our personal brands are continually being built. Whether it is done with intent, structure, and wisdom is a personal decision.

characteristics of your target audience

Possessing an understanding of promotional patterns, spending patterns, award patterns, or whatever exchange you will be making with your target is primary.

For example, if you are a music artist and you want to win an award, you need to understand the requirements for winning that award, you need to find out who has won the award in the past, and you need to know what they did or what kind of music do they make for them to win the award.

If you want a promotion on your job, you should find out:

- What qualifications are they looking for in this position?
- What skills do I have that fit this position, or what experiences do I have that can be substituted for a skill?
- What is the educational and work experience background of those who have held the position before me?

Knowing where you are and what you need helps connect you with your target.

notes

* * *

sample brand strategy

We are now going to provide you with the framework for an older version of my personal brand strategy. This is also the framework the contributing authors use as they are building their personal brands; therefore, it can be used to assist you as you develop your personal brand. You should not just be building, but you should have a solid strategy to follow.

TARGET:

Women who want to increase their prayer lives, identify their purpose, and begin to live in their purpose.

COMPETITORS:

Sarah Jakes Roberts, Priscilla Shirer, Chrystal Hurst

brand analysis (swot):

STRENGTHS: One hundred percent creative control, have authored several books and have prior speaking experience, low overhead costs (no large team), years of corporate and ministry experience.

WEAKNESSES: limited traffic as they have a lesser-known reputation, conservative churches only wanting to purchase from or book prominent name authors and speakers.

OPPORTUNITIES: hometown support and speaking engagements can join toastmasters to improve speaking, can enroll in marketing courses to improve marketing strategies, can put together book tours.

THREATS: Competitors have a larger team to help them execute their vision, competitors have a larger marketing budget to help them reach more people, or competitors have a greater reputation.

CHARACTERISTICS OF TARGET:

Targets require books that are inspirational, encouraging, life-changing, and at times, denominationally accurate. They spend between $18 and $30 on books that help with spiritual growth and development. My books should be priced accordingly — if the page count is appropriate — and the content should be engaging.

TARGET AVATAR:

Lisa is a thirty-five-year-old single woman living in Northern Louisiana who works as a Certified Nursing Assistant with a yearly salary of $30K. She spends her social media time on Facebook. Her goal is to elevate her prayer life, increase her income, and become more stable. She wants to save money to move away from the small town. She needs encouragement as she desires a life of abundance and opportunities.

To accomplish her goals, Lisa needs spiritual stability and mentorship. She would also like to add a stream of income. However, based on her current situation, she is not equipped to reach her goals, due to the lack of mentors and entrepreneurial resources available in her area.

How can I help Lisa? I can start by explaining the benefits of my book and how it will educate her and provide encouragement and tips to help her become more spiritually stable. I will explain how reading the content in my books is like one-on-one mentoring, except in literary form.

I understand that offering Lisa a product or service that is low cost will get her use to my brand experience; from there, she can decide if she wants to use me to help her create an additional stream of income and build a personal brand through authorship as a higher-cost service. It would not be wise for me to offer Lisa my self-publishing consulting services that cost a few thousand dollars. As brand personalities, we must look at a person's salary.

This is not to say we can determine what a person can afford, but it makes us more sensitive to offering them a high-ticket service. By starting Lisa off with my book, she can decide whether she wants to invest in other services. This also allows her an opportunity to save up for the self-publishing service if she is interested in my help to create an additional stream of income.

BRAND CHANNELS:

Effective ways to market my books, speaking, and self-publishing services are:

Facebook (this is where my target spends most of her social media time. You also want to market where your target spends most of their social media time. Although I am not a fan of social media, the focus is not on me. The focus is on where Lisa hangs out.)

Instagram (initially, you may want to focus on one platform, but as you grow, you will want to have a secondary platform. The secondary platform should be based on the second platform that the target spends time on. For example, if it were YouTube, I would spend time there; if it were LinkedIn, then I would spend time there.)

Professional Organizations and *Networking Groups* (this should always be a channel. Relationships are like currency. Where and with whom you spend your time will lead to connections and opportunities.)

Word of mouth (previous client testimonials.)

BRAND PERSONALITY:

Decide how you want to come across to your target. What image do you want them to hold in their mind about you? This is where voice, tone, and values come into play, meaning that your post should fit within this personality. A key to remember here is that there is more to it than what you post on your social media; it is also what you like, share, and comment on. It becomes a part of your brand personality.

When posting, liking, sharing, commenting, ask yourself, "Does this fit into my brand tone, voice, or values?" Be authentic, be personable, and have fun, but be mindful that if you are building a clean brand image, you should not be commenting, liking, and sharing harmful posts containing a lot of cursing, violent, sexually explicit content. No, you may not have been the one who posted it, but if you like it or share it, you are saying that you agree with it.

Voice and tone: Knowledgeable, graceful, patient, modern verbiage, serious, professional

Brand values: inspirational, encouraging, passionate, spiritual, prayerful

Decide on your voice, tone, and values. This is a basic part of your strategy.

UNIQUE SELLING PROPOSITION:

Do not confuse this to mean that this should only be included in your brand strategy if you are selling a product. When you are building a personal brand as a student, employee, or community leader, you are selling *yourself*. Determining what makes you different and unique from others doing the same thing is your unique selling proposition. Though it is remarkably similar, each of us brings value to who we serve.

Think about my female competitors. They are all powerhouse Christian teachers, speakers, and preachers. They have all published terrific books. They all have large followings and speak on grand stages. So, on the surface, it looks like I do not compare or measure up to them. They have significant platforms, millions of followers, and have done tremendous work in the marketplace and kingdom.

Nevertheless, I am also a female Christian speaker, teacher, and preacher with many books just like them. And although I have considerably fewer followers and have spoken on much smaller stages, here is what makes me unique and where I fill the gap: I have acquired the skill of self-publishing and helping women build a personal brand through authorship, adding a stream of income to their finances. I am not only able to provide mentoring and spiritual growth through my books and teaching, but I can empower women to add a stream of income by becoming published authors.

That is the lane that God created for me. That is the space He wants me to hold — a different and unique space from my competitors. So, after discovering my unique selling proposition and value, I stopped focusing so much on the traditional "speak, preach, teach" and realized that my dominancy was that I have a writing and prayer ministry. The teaching, speaking, and preaching are by-products of the core thing that God has called me to do.

It took me a while to embrace that because I thought being an evangelist meant my brand needed to look like it has always traditionally looked.

God repeatedly told me, "It does not take away you being anointed. I have called some to the church to equip the body; I have called you to the marketplace to equip the body. It is going to look different for everyone." Understand your value, what you bring, and where you are supposed to serve. Then, build your brand accordingly.

Brand Benefits:

You absolutely must be knowledgeable and capable of

articulating the benefit of collaborating with you, hiring you, having you in their program, having you in their class, having you as a part of their community group, or whatever your lane is. Understanding your unique value and being able to tell people about your value is beneficial for *you*; However, to get them to take action, you must also communicate what is beneficial for *them*.

What are your brand benefits? Following are some examples:

Randall, Sr. brand benefits: You will get quality t-shirts that are competitively priced. You will receive motivation and inspiration by having a life strategy session.

Cha'Darius brand benefits: You will get a combination of education and street knowledge by engaging in a conversation. This makes you diverse in your thinking and decision-making. You will get real and raw music that teaches a life lesson on the struggles of young, black faces and how they persevere through those struggles.

Randall, Jr. brand benefits: You will get quality merchandise and an inspirational conversation that will cause you to want to persevere. You will get real and raw music that demonstrates perseverance.

RaTiage brand benefits: You will be encouraged to think innovatively. You will get to see an appreciation of life, arts, and technology through his music, visuals, and promotional skills.

Pamela brand benefits: You will get books and speeches that educate and inspire women to grow spiritually, personally, and professionally. You will receive services that help women of faith build their personal brand through authorship while creating an additional income stream for their finances.

BRAND STORY:

Why do you do what you do? What passion or problem led you to be obedient to what God has called you to do so that you can impact others?

As an example, Pamela started writing as a hobby when she was a child, started journaling to release emotions as a teenager, and then began using writing as a ministry tool as an adult. While being teased as a child for choosing to read and write over playing outside, Pamela found passion in writing and praying.

She was often told that her voice was so soft and repeatedly asked if anyone took her seriously until she started to resent the sound of her voice. This added to her introversion but later became the very thing that God would use as a voice for breakthrough, inspiration, and empowerment.

Over time, she began to use her writing voice and her audible voice and started self-publishing her own books and speaking, which later turned into her helping other women (and a few men) self-publish their books and amplify their voices.

BRAND VISION:

What do you see yourself doing on a larger scale?

BRAND MISSION:

What is the reason you do what you do and how are you actively doing it?

BRAND TAGLINE:

What is a phrase or keyword by which your personal brand can be identified? For example, mine is "Books Build Brands." This became my tagline after seeing the benefit and the doors and opportunities that opened for me after becoming a published author. It was a book that started the development of my personal brand.

BRAND DESIGN:

Having a brand design, such as certain colors and specific font types, can polish your brand. We will not dive much into this as this complements your personal brand

and not the brand itself. Many get caught up in this part of the brand and think that starting a brand is colors, fonts, and websites. No, you can build a powerful brand without these elements.

Think about the people before us who we still honor today because of the personal brands that they built without these elements. These things are okay to have yet are not where the focus should be. You need all the other aspects of a brand except for a brand tagline and brand design — these two things are optional.

BRAND EXPOSURE:

This is the channel or channels by which your brand will become visible and spread. For each of these, you will need a marketing strategy.

- If you are a student, you can gain brand exposure by joining student associations and organizations; being active in them, using your voice, and offering innovative ways to make student life and success better.

- If you are an employee, you can gain brand exposure by volunteering for extra projects or sharing your best practices during meetings for how you manage your workflow and have great productivity.

- If you are an entrepreneur, you can gain brand exposure by sharing your wins and lessons, taking others through your entrepreneurial journey, and sharing customer testimonies and feedback.

- If you are a ministry leader, you can gain brand exposure by sharing what God has brought you through and helping others receive a breakthrough.

- If you are a community leader, you can gain brand exposure by being a community advocate and actively participating in projects, elections, and community meetings that have influence.

- If you do not fall into any of the above categories, you can still gain brand exposure by showing kindness and being helpful to those you see in passing and by becoming involved in your community, schools, or organizations.

There are other parts of the brand strategy specific to what you are doing, such as a marketing budget, the strategy to execute on everything laid out, and how you measure the growth of your personal brand. Remember, your personal brand strategy will become the blueprint by which you elevate your life and make a massive impact.

conclusion

It is critical that Black faces are seen and represented. We know it sounds cliché, but representation matters. As emerging Black leaders, creatives, authors, and artists, it is encouraging to see other black faces making moves and being accomplished. This does not mean that what you do has to be on a large scale as a celebrity. No matter what scale it is on, it is equally outstanding.

Seeing accomplished black faces is inspiring, and it is hopeful. For so many years, we have been discouraged and disheartened because we do not see many black faces leading in many industries and spaces. However, you can contribute to increased representation by building your personal brand. We know that we are innovative, talented, and created, and, unfortunately, we must work harder to prove it, but we must continue with the work that was started before us.

Although progress is being made, it is not being made at the rate that we would like to see, but we also have a

CONCLUSION

responsibility to try to close the gap by doing our part. Even if others do not embrace us, we should embrace each other as a community. No matter what has been spoken over us, no matter what has been believed about us, we were born to lead, and we are just as capable as anyone else.

Black faces can create, make a difference,
and help to change the world.

Personal brand building is a continuous thing. It is a part of personal and professional development. Still, it is something to be proud of and intentional about if we want to continue to claim our stake in society.

Let us continue to have self-worth. Before we can consider any accomplishment or accolade bestowed upon us by peers, social media, or society, we must feel good about who we are. We are Black, and that is something to be proud of. Because the truth is, we will never measure up to the changing standards and hypocrisy of society, having a sense of self-worth and a positive sense of self must be one of the core values by which we build. We are worthy simply because of who we are and not because of what we have done . . . or will do.

We must be authentic. We are living in a social media-dominated era. We have so many teachers and influencers on social media, so at any given second, we will have someone telling us how we should show up. As determined black faces, if we show up any other way than

CONCLUSION

who we truly are, we have failed - not only ourselves but also our culture. Sure, there will be certain trends that make sense for your personal brand, but remaining authentic is what makes a brand solid. We must continue to learn. We do not know it all. We will never know it all, but learning should be looked upon as a self-investment and one that any serious leader is willing to make. This will help us to continue to elevate and be empowered. It will help us to continue to rise above the adversity and the roadblocks designed to deter us.

Having a clear purpose helps us with our personal brand. One black person thriving in an area does not mean that **is** the area that all black people will thrive in. We must stop entering lanes that we have not been equipped to drive in. Staying in alignment with self-purpose helps us contribute to the community as a whole; that is how we become a united, resilient force. There will be many assignments attached to our individual purpose, but once we are clear on purpose, we become passionate about serving.

We should not shy away from opportunities. It does not matter how many doors have been slammed in our face; we have the power and the resources to create our own opportunities. Being that opportunities for us do not just flow from Wonderland, we must be proactive about it. Building our personal brands and developing as leaders requires us to market ourselves, highlight our expertise, and highlight our excellent skills and talents.

CONCLUSION

It does not matter what we are creating — art, music, technology, books, or babies — we are leaders, and building our personal brands helps us be seen as leaders.

Let us not bury ourselves by shying away from opportunities or failing to create our own. It's time to come out from underneath the ashes that have been laid on us to cover our greatness.

Black faces... we have what it takes to help change the world, lead others, and start a movement. We look forward to seeing you put your skin in the game as you build your personal brand.

resources

Roepe, Lisa Rabasca (2021). Barriers for Black Professionals www.shrm.org/hr-today/news Retrieved March 6, 2022.

Kauflin, Jeff (2017). Only 15% of People Are Self-Aware-Here's How to Change www.forbes.com Retrieved February 28, 2022.

Darling-Hammond, Linda (1998). Unequal Opportunity: Race and Education www.brookings.edu Retrieved March 17, 2022.

Opara, Ijeoma Dr. (2022). Tackling Disparities in Finance for Black and African Americans www.moneygeek.com Retrieved March 17, 2022.

about the authors

ABOUT PAMELA D. SMITH

Pamela D. Smith is an award-winning, best-selling, multi-published author helping corporate women of faith build memorable brands through authorship while helping them to grow spiritually, personally, and professionally. Helping women build brands so that they can excel in life, business, ministry, and career is at the core of what she does. Through brand building, she helps women amplify their voices in a noisy world.

Purposefully teaching, mentoring, empowering, and equipping while praying with women to become all they were created to be are among the many things that Pamela is doing.

Her brand-building journey began with herself with the release of her first self-published book. Since then, she has written eight other books, been a co-author in two books, been the Visionary Author in a family book collaboration, and is now the Visionary Author of Black face.

Her book, *While at the Altar*, won a Literary Titan Award. Pamela has been a Pink Carpet Award Honoree at La'Shae's Business Expo, received the Deborah Rising Marketplace Ministry Award, been named Author of the Year by K.I.S.H Magazine, named one of eleven women in Marketplace Ministry to watch in 2021 by Sheen Magazine, and a 2022 Mover and Shaker by Sheen Magazine. She has been featured in several magazines, podcasts, and online publications.

Pamela is a Licensed Minister and has an Undergraduate Degree in Social Science and a Master of Business Administration Degree.

To book Pamela to speak or request one of her services, go to www.pameladsmith.net. Follow Pamela on Instagram at @pameladsmith1

ABOUT RANDALL R. SMITH, SR.

Randall R. Smith, Sr., is the creator of the Black face brand t-shirt line and services. He is passionate about equal rights for black faces and encouraging others to push through. He has received his Bachelor's in Business Management and is often looked upon for an encouraging word. Randall plans to combine the t-shirt and book to expand the Black face brand.

Follow Randall, Sr. on Instagram at @blackfacebrand

ABOUT CHA'DARIUS L. SPENCER

Cha'Darius, aka "Base," is the father of one son and is an independent music artist and content creator. He has some college experience but was led to pursue his entrepreneurial endeavors in music and creating content. He has experience performing on stages and opening for A-list artists.

He plans to use this book and his music to continue to build his personal brand and empower his community. Cha'Darius is often looked upon for thought-provoking insight as he believes that knowing what is going on around you is the key to being a problem solver and an advocate for your community. His music is available on all streaming platforms.

Follow Cha'Darius on Instagram at @_ggbase1400

ABOUT RANDALL R. SMITH, JR.

Randall R. Smith, Jr., aka "June Bandero," is an independent music artist and content creator with a passion for being a resource to those around you. He has some college experience but was led to pursue an entrepreneurial path with merchandise and music. He has experience performing on stages and opening for A-list artists.

He plans to use this book, his music, and merchandise to continue building his personal brand.

Randall is looked upon for inspiration as he believes in sharing his life and business lessons with those around him. His music is available on all streaming platforms.

Follow Randall, Jr. on Instagram at @ggbandero_1400

ABOUT RATIAGE J. SMITH

RaTiage J. Smith, aka "Three," is an independent music artist and digital content promoter. As the father of one son, he is enthusiastic about learning technology and ways to invest in becoming a source of economic empowerment through education. He has experience performing on stages and plans to use this book and his music to continue building his personal brand and digital promotion services.

RaTiage is looked upon for his savviness in technology and educational information on investment news.
His music is available on all streaming platforms.

Follow RaTiage on Instagram at @ratiag3

For Assistance with a Personal Brand Strategy,
visit: www.pameladsmith.net

www.ingramcontent.com/pod-product-compliance
Lightning Source LLC
Chambersburg PA
CBHW050305120526
44590CB00016B/2502